# The

# E.M.B.R.A.C.E.

# FORMULA

7 STEPS TO SILENCING

THE ENEMY &

THE INNER ME

THE E.M.B.R.A.C.E. FORMULA

THE E.M.B.R.A.C.E. FORMULA

ALL RIGHT RESERVED © 2020

**Dorissa McCalister-Carnell**

ISBN: 13-9781735096104
LIBRARY OF CONGRESS: 2020908933

**FIRST PRINT USA**

# THE E.M.B.R.A.C.E. FORMULA

# DEDICATIONS

**God**, thank you for loving the most unlovable parts of me. Thank you for loving me despite myself. Thank you for always working things out for my good.

**Jesus**, thank you for taking my place. Thank you for living a life that modeled what a real servant looks like. Thank you for being my BFF.

**Daddy and Momma** (Oscar & Joe Francis McCalister), when God gave me you, He gave me His earthly best. #SeeYaLaterAlligators

**Khanlin and Kylea**...my pride and joy...my diamond and pearl...the two halves of my heartbeat. Momma loves you both...to the moon and beyond.

**Lisa**, You and me, Us never part
Makidada (Little Sister)
You and me, Us have one heart
Ain't no ocean, ain't no sea
Keep my Sistah 'way from me
Makidada

**Uncle Al and Aunt Julia**, you've blessed me with the gift of having you as "Stepped-In" parents, and for that, I'm so grateful.  With all my heart, I love you both.

**FranzellI**, Joe Francis only birthed two, but I couldn't ask for a more God-loving, compassionate, servant-hearted, and kind Big Sistah...you're my "Tukie".

**Calvin**, you're probably going to kill me when you read this, but it doesn't matter...I run faster than you, lol. You're always there for me, so I just want you to know how much I love and appreciate you, Bruh-Bruh.

**Bernard**, you are my listening ear, and voice of reason. I can always count on you to keep it real, then give me, your Lil Sis, words of wisdom. Thank you for consistently giving me the most priceless, but yet most valuable gift...the Word of God. I love you, Big Bruh Bishop Bernard (B4).

# ACKNOWLEDGMENTS

"I thank you all for your love, prayers and support. It makes my heart smile knowing I have you in my corner." - Dorissa

Karen Silmon

Brenda Palmer

Mia Johnson

Sophia Campbell

Trissi Jenkins

Vanell Vincent-White

Paulette Winston-White

Idele Joiner

Demetria (Dee) Anderson

Demetha Williams-Hunt

Lorice Harrison

Paula Johnson-Shelton

Lisa McCalister-Proaps

Ret. Col. Albert and Mrs. Julia Lamons Sr.

Regina Anderson

Stevii Aisha Mills

Taurea Avant

Stacy Walker
Facebook: Stacy Annette

Charnika P. Elliott
Noah-Christian Academy, www.noah-
christianacademy.org
www.charnikapelliott.com

Jeri Darby (Author, speaker, Writing
Coach)
Facebook: Jeri Darby,
Twitter: IamawriterNow  (989)402-4721

Staci Stills, MS, BSN, RN, AAFA, GEX
FITmom Moves
Facebook/Instagram/Periscope/Twitter:
FITmom Staci

Prophetess Leticia Lewis
Majestic Ministries International,
www.majesticmi.org

GRAND RISING QUEEN
Lovenia "Coach Love" Barkley

Keepsake Motivation,
www.keepsakemotivation.com

# FOREWORD

By Stevii Mills

I am so Godly excited to have been invited to write this Foreword! As you read this book you will find that you can feel Dorissa's energy leap from the pages. If you have ever heard her speak you know that her voice is one that is melodic, caring, inspirational and educational. That is what this book is too.

I love that she has given us this so that we can keep the EMBRACE formula top of mind. This is not just a book indeed it's a way of live. Personal Development is key to success and Dorissa has invited us all to enter into the realm of growing greater by giving us this easy to implement formula. She has broken down the complexities of what could possibly be hard to do and is guiding us through a journey of elevation.

I know that I will have this book close to me forever because I am ever evolving and want to be prepared for each and every step along my journey. I hope yeah you will do the same.

Stevii Aisha Mills, MS

Visibility Coach

www.howtomakeittothenews.com

# FOREWORD
by Marilyn E Porter

I am a *word* girl – I enjoy words, I enjoy all the vast possibilities that we can create with words. I love the way they sound and the way they can make us feel, especially a word like **EMBRACE**. Here a few meanings of the word:

- to take or clasp in the arms; press to the bosom; hug
- to take or receive gladly or eagerly; accept willingly
- to avail oneself of
- to adopt (a profession, a religion, etc.)

From the above we can see that **EMBRACE** is a verb – an action word. We can embrace a person physically, we can embrace an idea, and we can embrace opportunities of all kinds. Don't you just love this word!

As a child I learned in my 3rd grade Language class that one word can have various meanings, thus we must sometimes use context clues to be sure that we are following the flow of the conversation properly. One wrong missed clue and our entire perception can change – more often than not, it is changed in a negative manner. What have absolutely come to love about Dorissa – the fabulous author of this book – is that she is perception agitator but the goal is the change our perception from a negative to a positive – which ain't easy in this world that we reside in. BUT she has done right here in the pages of The E.M.B.R.A.C.E. Formula.

The world needs agitators and shifters – God knows I do and God and ME, know that you do too. So, I want you to prepare your heart and mind to be served by her words and to be shifted by her heart for God and His people. Clear you mind for just a moment and accept that your perception may be off in an area of your life. Maybe you've believed a lie, or you are the liar. Maybe you been selfish with others or not self-full enough for yourself. There are so many self-reflective areas to look at and this book is going to help you do just that – reflect on self. Get ready!

Sometimes it's not the other person.

Sometimes it's not the job.

Sometimes it's not where you live.

Sometimes it's not your Momma'nim.

Sometimes, MOST times, life can become more fulfilling with a minor mindset adjustment. Yes, a change is your perception of a thing.

Dorissa, The Perception Chick is serving it for you right here in the pages of this book! Sit back and relax and prepare to be ye transformed!

READY!

SET!

GO!

Peace and blessings to you all and Dorissa, I thank you for your contribution to making this world a better place for us all.

Marilyn E Porter

Overseer and Founder

The Pink Pulpit International Convention of Women in Ministry

www.marilyneporter.com

# THE E.M.B.R.A.C.E. FORMULA

# THE CONTENTS

# THE E.M.B.R.A.C.E. FORMULA

# INTRODUCTION

My Dear Sister,

I'm so proud of you! I'm happy and excited that you are taking your very first important step to embracing your life and seeing yourself through a loving God's eyes. If you're reading this book, like me, you've probably had to endure many life-altering, traumatic experiences.

**Were you abandoned at an early age?**

**Where you molested or raped?**

**Did you witness an injustice, but feel you didn't do enough to prevent it?**

**Were you passed up for a promotion you worked long and hard to obtain?**

**Did a spouse leave you for another?**

**Is someone constantly reminding you of how inadequate you are?**

**Were you teased and tormented as a child? As an adult?**

I've had experience in many horrific things myself, so I can honestly say that I can empathize with you and how you may feel as a result of those experiences.

**Do you feel...**

   **Angry?**

   **Ashamed?**

   **Unloved?**

   **Frustrated?**

   **Not enough?**

   **Unattractive?**

   **Ugly?**

   **Alone?**

   **Stupid?**

   **Unwanted?**

   **Abandoned?**

   **Unworthy?**

Is there one feeling that stands out the most, or do you identify with more than one? Either way, I can relate to how you may feel. For too long, I had listened to the conversations in my head that stem from the traumatic experiences I've had to live through. But you know what? One morning God interrupted my thought process and whispered to me that I didn't have to live with shame, anger and all the other emotional baggage that I'd been carrying around...and neither do you!

I've written this book for two reasons. The first is that people have always inquired as to how I keep a positive outlook so consistently, even when my life is under attack (which seems to happen quite frequently). The second, and most important reason, is because there was a time in my life where I believed everything Satan told me about myself. The "Inner Me" joined forces with "The Enemy" and the "war" in my mind had begun. I was 9 when I was molested in church, while there for Easter Sunday service speech rehearsal, and the enemy told me I had deserved it. When I was 22, I was pulled into a bathroom stall and raped on my college campus, and Satan told me no one would ever want me. I was blessed with the most loving Daddy, but he was murdered, during church service, by the pastor, and Satan told me that that was my last shot at ever being loved by a man. I've filed bankruptcy and lost a car, and the enemy told me I wasn't ever going to have anything. While being the sole caregiver of my Momma (who lived with Alzheimer's, and with me for 10 years), I watched her slowly slip away from me, all the while the enemy told me I wasn't enough for either of my parents to "stay" with me. I was blessed with a beautiful daughter who was born mentally and physically challenged, and Satan told me it was my fault. Lies, lies, lies, and more lies.

I believed them all for the majority of my life. Then one early morning, the Lord revealed something to me...the idea of changing my perception of what I had experienced in life from what I see with my limited vision, to what He sees with His all-knowing eyes. My friend, it changed my entire life. I believe that how you see your life, dictates how you approach and maneuver through your life. When I changed my perception, my entire life changed. When I stopped listening to the lies of Satan, and applying the truth (the Word of God), my entire life became incredibly satisfying. I want you to experience the joy of this transformation, too. I believe you can have the same thing, a happier, more fulfilling life, if you silence the enemy and his lies and listen to what God says about you. In this book, I am going to share with you all the steps God gave me that early morning...the morning that changed my life, so you too can embrace your life, embrace your purpose, and make peace with your past by seeing your life through God's eyes. So please take your time and read each chapter, then re-read it, taking notes along the way.

THE E.M.B.R.A.C.E. FORMULA

# E

# ELIMINATE

## YOUR INNER CHIT-CHAT

Commit to a different way of thinking.

Sometimes we don't know when to shut up

and when to listen. And that's the case

when it comes to quieting the chatter in our

minds.

The chatter of "You're not good enough".

The chatter of "You should be ashamed of

yourself". The chatter of "Nobody loves

you". That chatter, negative thoughts, and negative dialogue that are going on in your head is the voice of the enemy, Satan. He's always willing, ready, and more than able to whisper not-so-sweet nothings in your ear. Satan's job is to steal, kill and destroy. That's what he does. He never sleeps or slumbers. He's on the job 24/7, 365, no vacations. And although he doesn't have the power to control what you do, think or say, he does have a mighty weapon in his arsenal that he uses on a daily basis. It is one of his main weapons of choice (along with "shame"). That weapon is the power of suggestion. He's constantly whispering things in your ear, contrary to the Word of God. Never the truth, because the truth isn't in him. He's unable to tell the truth. Our problem is we engage him by listening, and we listen to him much longer than we should. We give him entirely too much space in our heads, and that can lead to trouble. As my grandmother used to say, "If you let him ride, eventually he'll want to drive", meaning, if we let him get comfortable "riding" in our minds too long, he will eventually take the wheel, and single-handedly control our thoughts. Before you know it, he will have given himself the title of designated driver, and owner of the "car" (your mind/thoughts). In order to embrace all that is "you", you must commit to changing the way you think about yourself, and that means starting with shutting Satan up, and shutting him down. It's important that you don't hesitate in taking control of our thoughts. You must commit to a different way of seeing yourself, as if your life depends on it, because it does. The thoughts that pertain to how you perceive yourself, will dictate how you maneuver throughout your life. Every decision, action, and reaction you experience in your life, will be in direct correlation to how you feel about, and see yourself. Once and for all, you must commit to silencing the negative, outright lies that Satan insists you buy into. You must commit to changing the rhetoric and making the truth (what God says) your new mantra.

*EVICTION* notice served! It's important to identify Satan and his tactics, so it will be easier for you to take him out of the equation.

It's time to evict Satan from your head space and serve him notice! It's time to let him know that you mean business, and that he's got to go! Let Satan know that even though he uses the power of suggestion, he cannot control your thoughts. Let him know that you're not falling for the ol' okey-doke. If you decide to take control of your negative perception of yourself, Satan will not be able to continually invade your mental space and disrupt your ability to believe what God says about you. It's time for you to end his stay and discontinue his reign. The Bible tells us that we have the power to rebuke the enemy (just like Jesus did) and he will obey our command. It's important to note here that simply using the phrase "I rebuke you Satan, in the name of Jesus", is not enough. That is not how you rebuke Satan. When you say, "I rebuke you, Satan", and even add "In the mighty name of Jesus", you are simply doing nothing more than telling the enemy what you are doing. Allow me to explain. Imagine I have a puppy who was sitting in the middle of my bed while tearing up my favorite pillow. I walk into my bedroom, catching him in the act, and I say, "I'm yelling at you", the puppy then stares back at me as if to say, "Yeah...and?" Instead, I should have said, "Get out of my bed...NOW!" In my first example, I simply made a statement to the puppy, but in the second example, I gave him a command.

Like with the puppy, we must give Satan a direct command. For instance, "Get out now", "Let go of my finances", or "Stop bothering my child". We must tell him EXACTLY what we want him to do, and how we want him to do it. You must then remind him that he has NO control. Take control over your thought-life today. Ask God to help you, then give Satan a few direct commands: "Stop talking to me", "Get out of my thoughts", and "Let go of my mind", and "Take your opinions of me, and shove it" (OK, that's not biblical, but it does make me feel really good saying it to him, lol).

**EXPECT** a fight from the enemy as you learn how to recognize the enemy's resistance.

Now don't get it twisted. The enemy is not going to cooperatively vacate the premises of your mind. He is going to put up a fight because he does not want to lose the control that he's always had over your life. Trust and believe, he is going to fight you tooth and nail, and he's not going to play fair. He will go as far as making you feel guilty for thinking you have the right to take control over your thoughts. He's going to suggest that you don't have the right to feel good about yourself. He's going to distract you with "memory-suggestions" that bring back feelings of shame, and shame is another one of the powerful weapons that he will use against you. If he can get you to feel ashamed of something you said or did, or if he can convince you that you should wear a cloak of shame because of something someone else said or did to you, he has you right where he wants you. You see, Satan doesn't like the idea of you listening to God's words, more than you listen to his suggestions. He's going to be downright angry when you try to change your perception and start to embrace yourself and all that is "You". So, beware.

Satan is very crafty in communicating negative messages. He'll do just about everything in his power to keep you from getting on the right train of thought. One of his tactics is he will try to distract you, and he'll do it by attempting to overwhelm your thoughts with his suggestions. You can recognize his "clap-back", because he will soon start talking to you and whispering not-so-sweet nothings in your ear more frequently. He'll start immediately after you attempt to change your thought pattern. Oh yes, he's going to come at you hard, and he's playing for keeps. He won't be gentle or kind in his attack to win your mind.

Understand this, the best way to win a war, is to know your enemy, and if you study Satan, you will learn that he gets real nervous to the point he will flee, at the slight mention of Jesus and His words. You need to be "strapped", and geared up to fight your enemy. Geared up with the whole armor of God's word.

You must turn to scripture to effectively fight (rebuke) the enemy.

Satan is not your friend. He hates you. He wants to see you unhappy for the rest of your life, and it brings him great joy to know you spend days and nights crying. Satan is dedicated on destroying you. There is nothing more important to him than that, and that is why you must never forget who he really is, and how he feels about you. His life's mission is to lie to, kill, and destroy you. Period. Some say, "Stay ready, so you don't have to get ready", and it's good advice. You should always stay on alert, and be "weapon ready" (your weapon is the Word). Satan has very few tactics, but the one he seems to use the most are lies. Because he is the "Father of Lies", he is masterful at what he does. He can be ever so convincing. He has studied you your entire life and has seen everything that has happened in your life. Even the things that were never your fault, he has the uncanny ability to "Olivia Pope" the details, and make you feel shameful, guilty, and responsible for something that wasn't in your power. He uses the weapon of lies strategically and convincingly. The word of God is what you should be using as your weapon of choice. If you are to battle, you must be armed at all times, and that means you are to put on the whole armor of God according to Ephesians 6:13-17. The battle you are fighting against Satan is spiritual, not physical, so no tangible weapons are going to work against him. When you put on the whole armor of God, and apply it faithfully, you will be victorious against Satan. You must meditate on the Word, study it, memorize it, and live it, so when Satan rears his ugly little head, you can go at him full throttle, shouting the Word as your commands at him...straight no chaser, with no mercy, the same way he treats you. God gave us His Word to live by, and to instruct, correct, teach, comfort, and protect us. The battle between you and Satan is in your mind, and you have every right, as a child of the one and only true God, to win. And the only way to win is to use what God gave you, and that's His word. It's the only way you can go toe-to-

toe with your enemy, and win. Make it as your weapon of choice against Satan. You'll win every time.

# M

# MAKE

## A LIST ABOUT YOU

**Your past matters.**

To have a successful perception changing journey, you must

1. Take a long, hard look in the mirror, and ask yourself who you see when you look at your reflection, and

2. Be able to distinguish the enemy's lies from God's truth.

One of the hardest struggles you'll probably have to deal with when trying to completely change your perception of yourself, is conquering the need to fall into patterns of punishing yourself, and defining yourself based on your past mistakes, challenges, and decisions. Your past can weigh you down like an anchor around your neck, and the enemy is well aware of that. He will always be quick to throw your past in your face. Every chance he gets, he will drudge up your most painful memories, and distract you with them. In regards to those memories, he knows that you most likely have a great deal of unresolved hurt, guilt and shame (another one of his most used weapons), so he figures, what better way to keep you mentally in bondage, and blocked from receiving the truth of what God says about you. He thoroughly enjoys rubbing your pain in your face, and since he does, you have to do something drastic, by taking the next step towards mental freedom. Let's start by making a list of everything you can think of that you say to yourself, about yourself. And yes, you are to actually take pen to paper and write those things down.

Take a piece of paper and fold it lengthwise and then unfolded it. On the left side, write down the negative things that you believe about yourself. You can even add the negative things others have said about you. Write down everything that comes to mind. Don't think about it, just be spontaneous and write down the first things that pop in your head. Leave the right side of the paper blank after you're done. You will use it later after you've read chapters 4 and 5. After you have written the list, wait a few days to re-visit it. After a few days, you will reflect on the negative self-talk that you have participated in during the period spent since you wrote the list on the paper. Practice listening to yourself and try to capture every negative thought you have on paper. You will probably be surprised at just how many negative thoughts you write down.

So, what's your story?

**Your story matters**.

With every tear you've cried, every trauma you have experienced, and every defeating moment that has occurred, you were presented with an opportunity to

1) learn a positive and valuable lesson, or

2) concluded that it was all your fault
   that the whole situation occurred in
   the first place.

You may have decided, based on the
enemy's lies, that because you are not
worthy, pretty, or smart enough, you
surely deserve all the trauma that has
occurred in your life. All of the many lies
the enemy whispers in your ear, are just
that, lies. Every single time you
conclude that you are somehow to
blame, it will eventually become easier
and easier over time, for that way of
thinking to automatically become your
default mindset. If a parent abandoned

you, instead of seeing their blame, you will automatically conclude that you are somehow responsible. You may tell yourself you are unlovable, unwanted, and unworthy of security and dependable people in your life. If you are divorced, you may conclude that you are unattractive and undeserving of happiness and a strong, loving relationship. If you are single, you may conclude that no one will ever want to spend their life with you. My point is, when you have established a pattern of listening to Satan's lies, you become accustomed to drawing conclusions that are so far from the truth, it becomes your normal way of thinking. Why? Because the enemy is constantly practicing the art of reminding you of your situation and how you are to blame, and you keep practicing the art of believing his lies. He encourages your feelings of self-loathing, unworthiness, self-hate, and shame. In fact, he not only encourages it, he promotes it! He's your biggest cheerleader when it comes to your self-sabotage. He never wants to see you free from the me 'mental mess" you are presently entangled in, nor does he want to see you embrace the You God created. Satan is your enemy, and you should never forget that he'll do whatever it takes to keep you where you are. He knows that if you ever start paying more attention to God's word, or learn that you have power over the tricks he's played on you, and the lies he's told to you, the gig will be up, and so will the hold he thinks he has on you!

## Rumors

What you say about yourself, to yourself, matters. Just like what you believe others say about you matters. Why? Because your perception of something, and in this case, yourself, will dictate everything you do and say. I like to use the example of a person who sees themselves as fat or ugly. From the time they wake up, and get out of bed in the morning, to the time they lay their head on the pillow to go to sleep at night, everything they say and do, is dictated by their perception of themselves. Since they perceive themselves as fat and ugly, they will, more than likely when they get up in the morning, choose baggy clothes, as opposed to form fitting clothes that will show off their physique. Why? Because they more than likely want to hide themselves. They may choose to go through the fast food line and get two super-size combos, as opposed to eating a nice healthy salad. Why? Because they may have listened to Satan when he whispered, "It won't make a difference, you'll always be fat and ugly". They avoid social settings because they don't think they measure up to other people's standards. They may pass up opportunities to travel, get a job promotion or start a new business so they can live their best life, because they don't feel they are worthy. Why? Because they have somehow concluded that what the enemy has suggested they believe about themselves, is actually the truth. And to make matters worse, they create a support group of sorts, that "back up" and support everything the enemy suggests. Who are these people who make up the "support group"? They are any person who has uttered a negative word about you, to you...and that includes you. By allowing yourself to be influenced by the negative opinions of others, you are once again putting God's opinion of you, last (if at all). Now don't get me wrong, people will always have an opinion about you. No matter what good intentions you may have, no matter how kind, respectful, helpful and loving you are, or how hard you try to live your life as close to Jesus as possible, you must face the reality that you will never be everyone's cup of tea. Your opinion of yourself, when based on the opinion of others, will constantly change. Life experience has taught me that people's opinion of you can change from day to day, minute by minute, and depends on the current situation. That is why your perception of yourself can never be hinged on the opinion of others, including yourself, and it's wise to remember that, "Other people's opinion of you , is none of your business". Only God's opinion matters, because God's opinion is based on what is true (the Word), and the Word never changes. No one knows you better than He does, including yourself. He made you, and wrote your "owner's manual", because no one knows the creation better than the manufacturer Himself. He is your creator, and he knows every hair on your head, every tear you've cried, every mistake you've made...and He still loves you.

## Let's Just Call A Thang, A Thang

Satan tells lies, so he is a liar. Period. There's no other way to put it. He's a liar and the truth isn't in him. Everything he "says" to you is a lie. So how do you differentiate between the enemy's lies and God's truth? How do you learn to ignore the lies that keep you from loving yourself and seeing yourself through God's eyes? The one thing you should always remember is that Satan has a plan to destroy your life, just as God has a plan to bless your life. You must understand that the enemy wants you to remain stuck. Stuck in your fear. Stuck in your stress. Stuck in anxiousness. And most of all, stuck in your mess. In "The Mess" is where he prefers us to be because the truth is, misery loves company. The enemy knows that he is already defeated, but he will do everything in his power to keep us from recognizing this fact. That's why it is so easy for him to convince us that we are a lost cause. That our situation will never change. That we are not good enough. That we are unlovable. So, the original question was how do you differentiate the enemy's lies from God's truth? And the answer is, you go straight to the Word. It's that simple, because His Word is true. We need to stand on the Word, depend on the Word, study the Word, believe the Word, and apply the Word in order to fully benefit from it, and see a change in our mindset and perception. The truth is God loves us, and He has given us everything we need to overcome fear, stress, anxiety, unworthiness, shame, and our entire "mess".

# B

# BELIEVE

## What God Says IS TRUTH

What does the Bible say about you?

He created you – He's the manufacturer.

In an earlier chapter, we established that what you think of yourself, will dictate how you perceive and live your life. The importance you place on your value, is in direct correlation to your understanding of God's truth about you. If you don't place value on what God says about you, then there's no way you will place value on yourself. It kind of boils down to who are you going to believe? God's report about you or your own? Let me make my point by using a vacuum as an example. When you purchase a new vacuum cleaner and aren't quite sure as to how it works do you call a plumber? Do you call a chimney sweeper? No, neither one of these is an option. The only logical thing to do is to open up the manufacturers owner's manual, or call the company that made the vacuum. Why? Because who else would know the product better than the one who created it? If you want to know what the vacuum is capable of doing, and what features it has, you read the manual. If you want to know what it can and cannot do, you read the manual. Regardless of the opinions of the plummer, the chimney sweeper, or owners' of other brands of vacuums, no one knows or can tell you better about your vacuum than the manufacturer that created it. That is why the manufacturer is the only one whose opinion you can trust. The manufacturer is the only one who can tell you for which the product was made. The same applies to God our Father. He made us. He knows us, and even in our shortcomings, we are strong in Him! He created us with purpose, on purpose, and anyone else who says different, is just repeating what the enemy wants us to believe.

A lie is a lie, and a lie can't stand forever. Satan is the Father of lies. He's been telling lies since the beginning of time (remember Eve?) His whole entire existence is wrapped around his ability to lie, and get you to believe his lies. Hook line and sinker. *Lying is his native tongue.* Satan will have you believe that if there is no such thing as absolute truth, then there's no absolute lie...and that in and of itself is a lie! He has been twisting the truth since the beginning of time, and he won't be stopping anytime soon. He prowls around searching for someone, anyone, to lie to. Satan's lies have the power to destroy lives, and his primary goal in life is to destroy you. Long ago, he began a crusade to lead you to believe that he has more power than God, but that didn't fly for long, because sometime around 33 A.D., God sent His son, and He conquered it all...sickness, death and lies!

Satan lies about how you don't matter to God, but God says otherwise:

I John 4:9-10

"In this the love of God has made manifest among us, that God sent his only son into the world, so that we might live through him. And this is love, not that we have loved God but that he loved us and sent his son to be the propitiation for our sins."

Whatever Satan says or suggests to you, God has a direct response, and His response is truth. Nothing the enemy says will hold up. A lie cannot stand forever, but the truth, God's truth, will always prevail, and never come back void.

So, who will you believe? The one who hates you, and wants your dreams, goals, and relationships to die, or the one who loves you, died for you and puts you first? You have to make a choice because your very life depends on it. You have to choose not to listen to the enemy when he constantly bombards your mind with suggestions and lies about your powerlessness, your future, your ability to control your feelings, your happiness, and your life. You must choose to believe God, the one who created you in

His image. You must choose to believe God, the one who will always be your protector, your refuge, your deliverer, you healer, your provider, your friend, your Savior.

**God values you**. (see, John 3:16)

The world will have you think that you are only worth something if you are physically attractive, have lots of money and influence, possess a lot of material things, and have lots of awards on your wall. This is the world's way of thinking and also the enemy's lies. You are loved and valued by God simply because of who you are. Consider the fact that not only were you made in His image, and in His likeness, but when He was finished creating you, He said it is good, and the Bible tells me that He's incapable of lying. He shows that He loves you so much, that He takes the time to know every hair on your head. He knows every tear you have cried, and He knows every painful experience. How? Because He was with you the whole time. Because He never leaves your side. Because He's fighting your battles everyday. He knows you by name, and it's His intent that you live and prosper. He proved once and for all that He loves you, so much that He gave his only son to die an undeserving, public, excruciating death, just so that you can experience the gift of eternal life.

# R

# REPLACE

## YOUR LIST (ENEMY'S LIES)

## WITH GOD'S TRUTH

Mirror, Mirror on the wall...

Chances are, what you see when you look

at yourself in the mirror, is quite different

than what God sees when he looks at you.

Although God sees and knows all about you, He doesn't see you as a big, unnecessary ball of mistakes and failures. He is not ashamed of you. He loves you, in spite of your past. He loves you so much that even when He knew you'd make some bad choices, live recklessly and maybe even deny His love for you, He still chose to send His only son Jesus to die in your place. Jesus could have called a legion of angels to save him from the cross, but He didn't. He stayed because He loves you. He did it because he felt you were worth it. He chose to pay for all of your sins on that cross, so it's a done deal. God isn't judging your looks, or your weight, or imperfections, He simply sees you as His precious child. His beloved. He sees who you are in Christ, and the blood his son shed for you. When God looks at you, He sees his beloved son Jesus. He only sees the righteousness of His son Jesus Christ when He looks at you (1 Corinthians 1:30). When He sees you, He is looking at you through His eyes of blessings, forgiveness, love, and kindness.

YOU are NOT your past mistakes. (2 Corinthians 5:17) It's so tempting to let our past mistakes, decisions and sins keep us from living our best life, from being happy, from succeeding in life, and smiling at ourselves in the mirror. Every day we wake up to a new day, we're given a new chance, a fresh new start and a clean slate. Every new day is another opportunity to let go of the past, accept God's forgiveness, and see ourselves through God's eyes of forgiveness, compassion, and love. If You belong to Jesus, you have a brand new, sparkling, clean life in Him. Because you have asked God's forgiveness, He is faithful to forgive. And since He has forgiven you, then who are you to pull rank, and keep judging and punishing yourself, when He has already "hit the gavel" concerning the matter? Is your opinion higher than God's? Once God has forgiven you, you should do the same. Once again, let me remind you that you must get into the habit of shutting the enemy up. Tell him to leave you alone, release your thoughts and go bother someone else. As soon as you rebuke him by commanding him what to do, YOU must immediately replace whatever the enemy was suggesting to you, with the Word of God. God's truth will set you free.

## WHAT GOD SAYS ABOUT YOU

**You have purpose.** (Exodus 9:16) You are here for a reason and that reason is more than just your current hourly occupation. God has a great purpose for your life. He has numbered all of your days, and He will fulfill every purpose He has for you. The first (general) purpose for your life, is that you know, enjoy and fellowship with God. A big part of you knowing God, is you accepting what He says about you. You must know and believe what He says is true. The second purpose for your life is more specific. It has to do with all the unique characteristics, qualities, gifts, talents, and attributes God created in you. Identifying these are key to you knowing your purpose, because those qualities are the very things God will use for His purpose and desired outcome. Your purpose here on earth is to be as unique as you are.

**You are a masterpiece.** (Ephesians 2:10) God-created every living thing. He spoke the Earth, the universe, the stars, the planets, and every creature into existence. But with mankind He actually breathed the "Breath of Life". He gave us dominion over every living thing, and we are the only creation that He gave the power of free will, and the gift of eternal life (if we so choose).

We are His only creation to be made in His

image. And in the all the hundreds of

thousands of years of mankind's existence,

there have never been two people that are

just alike. Each person that has ever been

born is totally unique, and never to be

duplicated.    You are His masterpiece. A

one of a kind work of art. There has never

been, nor will there ever be another like

you. As cliché as it may sound, when He

made you, He broke the mold. You are His

precious child, and forever He will cherish

you.

**You are a diamond in the rough.** (Romans 5:8) You are a work in progress. You may not see it, but the things that are pressuring you, and the experiences that seem like the worst times of your life, are actually going to turn out to be the most treasured times in your life. Your rough patches in life sometimes make it convenient to stay paralyzed in the negative mental state you're in. In other words, you get comfortable in the uncomfortable. But in actuality, it's those seasons in your life that change you, and help change your mindset, making you a better version of yourself. Let's take the diamond for example. It's a beautiful precious stone coveted by many. But it doesn't start out that way. Did you know that a diamond is really a lump of coal that withstood pressure at extreme conditions and temperatures to evolve into the beautiful, light-reflecting stone that it is? Such is your life. You must constantly remind yourself that although there are imperfections in you and your life, God adores you, and all the beautiful flaws that are imperfectly perfect about you, including our story and how you came to be "You".

**You are loved unconditionally.** (Romans 8:38-39, Jeremiah 31:3, John 4:8) God's love for you is relentless, immeasurable, and infinite. People tend to love conditionally and put certain limitations, conditions, and requirements on their love for instance "I'll love you when..." or " I will only love you if...", but God's love is without restrictions or limits and it's unquestioning. God is the perfect source of love. There is nothing you can say or do that will cause God to love you any less. Granted He does not like sin, but He loves the sinner. The Bible tells us that nothing, no man, and nothing can ever separate us from His love. The enemy wants you to believe that God hates you, because you aren't a perfect person. Because you've made mistakes. Because there's been some bad decisions in your life. Or because you've caused harm to someone or something. And even though you have asked for forgiveness, Satan wants you to believe that nothing you can say or do will put you back in God's good grace. The truth of the matter is God loves the sinner, and not the sin, so when you ask for forgiveness, His love never changes. He is quick to forgive, and cast all your trespasses, into the sea of forgetfulness.

The problem is we don't do the same, we keep bringing up the same old mess, punishing ourselves, and believing in the enemy's lies. Why do we forget that God is love? That is who He is!

**You are a Conqueror.** (Philippians 4:13) The enemy will have you believe that your circumstances are greater than you are. That life is full of trouble, and there's no good in it. That you might as well quit. But God's word tells us otherwise. You are more than a conqueror! You can do anything, and all things through Christ! There will be times in your life that are difficult, and there will be times that you think you should give up. There will be times when you feel you are incapable of "getting life right". That is the time that you should remember that nothing is impossible with God. You may doubt yourself or think you are incapable of doing certain things, but God gives you the strength to do all things, and He is with you all ways. No matter what the challenge, if you trust in God and put Him first in everything you do, you will not fail, even with the things that you think are impossible. Nothing is impossible with Him. The key to knowing that you can do all things, is knowing that He is your secret weapon.

**The Old Switch-A-Roo...GET RID OF STINKIN-THINKIN!** It can be difficult to manage your negative thoughts, but it's not impossible. What comes out of our mouths typically starts with what's going on in our minds. If we meditate on negative thoughts long enough, they eventually become our patterns of behavior. In other words, our thoughts manifest themselves. A change in our negative thought patterns (thought patterns) does not start by changing our behavior, nor does it start by just "thinking positive". Yes, it helps to be intentional in surrounding yourself with positive people and things. It helps to detox your environment, circle of friends and contact list. But the real answer is in Romans 12:2:

"Do not conform to the pattern of this world, but be transformed by the renewing of your mind then you will be able to test and approve what God's will is his good pleasing and perfect will."

The key to conquering and ridding yourself of negative thought patterns, is not to rely on your own willpower, or your own understanding, but to rely on God to renew your mind. Yes, of course there are some things you must do, like concentrate on what is just, and pure, and lovely, and admirable, and surround yourself with things and people that are honest, and sincere, and positive, and loving. In doing this you won't have time to focus on the things that keep you in the mental prison of resentment, anger, self-doubt, bitterness, anxiety, fear, and other negative thought patterns. You must ask God for wisdom, and peace in your thoughts. His peace that surpasses all understanding. A peace that only God can give you. Never stop praying over your emotions and negative thoughts. And of course, apply God's word every chance you get.

# A

# APPLY

## AFFIRMATIONS

**Right the vision**.

The easiest way to get a visual of your negative thought patterns, is to write them down. When you write something down, that's when the magic happens. It makes what was confusing and difficult to comprehend and visualize, suddenly now crystal clear. Writing things down makes the idea, plan or description plainer, and easier to comprehend. After you write something down, you will be able to start reading it. When you start reading it, you can now start saying it out loud. When you start saying it out loud, you start hearing it and visualizing it in a different way. Once you start hearing it, you start to believe it. And when you get to the point you believe it, things begin to change. Note, that about this time, the enemy will start to "fall back" because he hates it when you start listening to God more than you listen to him. The more you practice writing down what God says about you and say them out loud, the more things begin to change, and you will start to understand and believe even more so, what God says about you.

Remember the list you made in chapter 2? According to scripture, the power of life and death is in the tongue (Proverbs 18:21), that is why you should watch what you say. When you speak negativity, you are speaking death upon yourself, your hopes, your dreams, your desires, and your self-esteem. Since the enemy is always looking for an opportunity to kill and destroy you and everything you have including your dreams, family, reputation, and health, it's best that you don't speak your negative thoughts out loud. Once you speak them out loud, it confirms to the enemy not only your state of mind, but how much work he has or doesn't have to do to destroy you. We make his job so easy for him by speaking our thoughts. We take the guesswork out of it for him. After we speak or negative thoughts out loud, all he has to do is respond accordingly to what we just said about ourselves.

THE E.M.B.R.A.C.E. FORMULA

**Hold a press conference.** Here is where you refer back to that list you made back in chapter 2. At times it seems like it's impossible to shut off the negative chitter-chatter in our minds. Some days, do you feel like the voice inside your head is so loud and contrary to how you really feel, it sounds like another person living inside of your head? Now that you know Satan is clocking your every move, are you thinking that from now on it's going to get more difficult to monitor your thought patterns day by day? Are you anticipating worrying about the enemy sharing your secrets to the world? Yes, he's cunning, and he knows that the last thing you want is for all of your business being discussed at the dinner table of everyone you know. Satan uses shame to keep you silent, feeling alone, undesirable, unwanted and unloved. But you have a weapon that's mightier than the cage the enemy tries to put you in. That weapon is your voice. May I suggest to you, that you hold a "press conference". That means, take the power from Satan telling your story, and tell it yourself. Use your voice to speak your truth, and your truth is what God says about you. Use your voice to tell your story. Tell your story for everyone to hear. Somebody needs to see and hear what a person who has lived their life condemning themselves, looks like now that they're free from the bondage of the enemy's lies.

**Believe** - Not just on Sunday and holidays, but you must believe in what the Word of God says about you all the time. It's not just a Sunday service kind of thing. It has to be a way of life – a committed event. There will be many times in your life where believing what the enemy says about you will be so easy to do, that's why you have to make up your mind and commit to believing early on. You must not give the enemy any opportunity to start his game of lies with you. It only takes one suggestion on his part, to lead you down a path of never-ending, self-destructive lies. You can't entertain him for a second. It's simply not worth it. Once you get silent and listen to him too long, he'll make another suggestion, then another, and before you know it, you're listening and entertaining him, more than you are meditating on what God's Word says about you.

**Be picky** - Watch the company you keep. It's important that you be selective about those you hang out with or consider

THE E.M.B.R.A.C.E. FORMULA

"friends". It's true that the people you have in your circle of friends tend to rub off on you. Many people believe the that we are all a direct reflection of our five (5) closest friends. That means we actually become like the five (5) closest friends, of which we spend the most time. If those five friends of yours speak negatively about everything including themselves, more than likely you will adapt to that way of thinking, also. If those five friends think they are unworthy, unlovable, and unattractive, you too will most likely accept these beliefs. This "Average of Five" principle is mentioned in the Bible:

"Do not be misled, bad company corrupts good character" (1 Corinthians 15:33). Take inventory. Who are the five people with whom you closely assemble? Can you think of ways that your speech resembles theirs?

# C

# CELEBRATE YOU!

**"I love Me" List** - Can you list 10 things that you like about yourself?

I love me, and today, I can say that honestly. There was a time when that wasn't the case. When was the last time you looked in the mirror, and sincerely said to yourself, "I love you"? Here's an exercise: Stand in front of a mirror, look yourself square in the eye, and say the words "I love you". How did it feel to say that to yourself? Was it uncomfortable? Did it feel weird? Why do you think that is? Were you able to look yourself in the eye? Let me share with you, something about myself.

For at least 30 years of my life, I was unable to look at myself in the mirror. I didn't notice this until I was about 40 years old. It was a Wednesday morning, and it was raining. I got up and ready to start my day of taking care of my Momma and daughter, who were both totally dependent on me. To this day, I remember the very second that I noticed that I was avoiding eye contact with my reflection in the mirror that was in front of me. I must say, it came as a complete surprise, as I noticed that I continued to avoid looking up at myself. The longer I stood there, the more uncomfortable I became. I started to brush my teeth and stared down at the sink while doing so. It dawned on me, that this is what I had done every single morning of my life, for all of my life. The longer I brushed my teeth, the longer I thought about the simple things I couldn't answer, like, what shade of brown were my eyes? Did I have any pimples that had showed up overnight? Did I look as tired as I felt? I couldn't even answer these questions, because I refused to look in the mirror. In fact, I couldn't answer the same questions as they pertained to the day before that, or the day before that, or the day before that. Wow. Really? The more I thought about it, the more I concluded that I seemed to have developed a habit of avoiding my reflection in the mirror for as long as I could remember. Every morning, when I would wash my face and brush my teeth, I would focus my attention to the drain in the sink, never the mirror. Every time I think about that morning, I cry for myself, on behalf of myself. I cry for the little girl inside who was always teased by the school bully at James Monroe Elementary School. I cry for her because she grew up to believe the lies that Satan had whispered to her (with the help of the "mean girl"). I still shed a tear for her/me, because so many years have been wasted believing She/I was ugly, unlovable, unworthy, and not enough. Those are the words that popped in my head when my eyes met mine for the first time in that mirror. Etched in my memory, is the moment I actually stood in front of the mirror, and made the decision to look at myself, and really see myself...the me God

THE E.M.B.R.A.C.E. FORMULA

sees. Granted it wasn't an easy decision to make, for I had attempted to do it several times before. But I knew I didn't want to live unhappy and depressed, any longer. I knew that there had to be a different and better way of perceiving myself. I wanted to embrace me, love me, accept me. I got to a point where I realized that my eyes and thoughts were playing tricks on me, but why? I wanted to change my perception of myself, but I didn't have a clue as to how to do that. It bothered me for days. I went nights without sleep because it kept me awake. Then It happened. It was Saturday, October 22, 2016, at approximately 2:15am

PST. I was up with my Momma, looking at old DVDs of "Everybody Loves Raymond" (one of her favorite shows), and the Lord impressed upon me, "Only what I say about you matters". "But what do you say about me, Lord?", I wondered. It took a second, but I finally had an ah-ha moment (Thank you, Holy Spirit). It was then that I knew that the only way I would know what God said about me, was to search for His words. I grabbed my phone, clicked on the **YouVersion** app, and confirmed the scripture he placed upon my heart, "You are wonderfully and beautifully made' (Psalm 139:14). I've heard this scripture many times throughout my life, but I never considered applying it to myself. That very night/morning, God inspired gave me eleven (11) affirmations. For someone who had never considered even looking at her reflection in the mirror, writing them came as easy as breathing. That was almost four years ago, and to this day, I have recited them daily.

I challenge you to search the scripture and write your own affirmations. Write them down, and put them on your bathroom mirror, so you can see and recite them every day. Carry them with you in your car.

Carry them with you during your long commute to work. Keep a copy in your purse to read while waiting in the doctor's office or DMV. Make them a screensaver on your phone or computer. Whenever you begin to feel bad about yourself because of something negative a "friend", a coworker, a relative, or even yourself, has said about you, pull it out, read it and celebrate yourself. Celebrate everything about yourself that once made you feel inadequate, unworthy, unloved, and not enough. Celebrate it all!

**Your strengths** make you special. It may be a little difficult (and maybe uncomfortable) to make a list of your own strengths, but it's something that must be done if you want to get a clear understanding of how you perceive yourself. You are special in every way, and when you compile your list of strengths, you will begin to see how you really see yourself. Find a quiet place where you will not be disturbed, then begin to write. Write down everything that pops into your head. Don't edit or second guess yourself, just write. Don't just list the obvious, like nice eyes, pretty smile, and gorgeous skin. List the things about you that aren't so obvious, like how creative, respectful, trustworthy patient, kind and loving you are. Remember the list you made in chapter two of all the negative talk you had with yourself? Now it is time to fill out the right side of the paper. For every negative thing you wrote down you are to find a scripture that counters it. Now some scriptures were given to you in chapter 4 but there's plenty more to be found. In fact, it's best that you research them for yourself, because they will have more meaning to you if you actually do your own research.

This is the first step to writing your own affirmations. Your affirmations are to be as unique as you are because they are a part of you rewriting your life story. For those of you who aren't familiar with the Bible, and don't know it word-for-word, that's ok. This is the perfect time to start getting acquainted with the Word of God. The more you read it, and search for answers, the more He will reveal to you. And let me let you in on a little secret. If you don't know anyone personally who can assist you in your search, there's this "little" company called "Google", and they have a search engine you can use for free to find just about everything. Yes, Mr. Google can be a friend in time of need! If one of the negative things you say to yourself is, "I am unworthy", then simply Google "What does the scripture say about feeling unworthy", or you can Google "What does scripture say about feelings of unworthiness?". Get it? Good, because you can't use "I don't know how" as an excuse to not take action against Satan...your enemy.

**Your experiences** and how they can help others. Have you ever stopped to consider the fact that your life is not your own? Have you ever thought that the things that you

have experienced in your life, were not only
for you, but for the betterment of others?
The enemy will have you believe that your
life has been a great big waste of time and
energy, but nothing can be further from the
truth. He wants you to think that nothing
you have ever been through has any value
or meaning in the large scheme of things.
That's a lie! God's Word says that "all things
work for the good of those who love the Lord
and are called according to His purpose"
(Romans 8:28). Notice it doesn't say
"everything IS good", it says that "it will all
work out FOR the good". No tear,
frustration, trial, tribulation, mistake, or

bad decision is a waste. Your life, with all of its ups and downs, good and bad, joy and pain, has purpose. Although it was probably painful at the time, your test is now your testimony.

You learned valuable lessons from your experiences, and when you share your story, you will help so many others. That's the beauty of coming out on the other side of a problem, crisis or traumatic event…you have a unique opportunity to bless someone else with your testimony. You experienced things that you thought were going to be the worst-case scenario of your life, but they turned out to be the best-case scenario. God always brings beauty out of an ugly situation. And his word he promises to give beauty for ashes (Isaiah 61:3). What you have to realize is, your life story and testimony, will be the very road map someone else needs.

**Your gift and talents = YOUR Purpose.** God has given you a talent, maybe many talents, and that is a blessing. How you use those talents is your choice, but know this, if you don't use it, you'll lose it (and that's straight scripture, Matthew 25). You may not be able to sing like Yolanda Adams, or be known worldwide like Oprah Winfrey, but you do have talent, and that gift or talent God gave you, was strategically chosen just for you. No matter who you are reading this chapter right now, I can guarantee that He is intentional about what He does, and that includes giving you certain gifts, talents, and experiences. Not sure you have a talent? Keep in mind your talent doesn't have to only be those things you see celebrated on TV, and in the movies. Consider the fact that you may have this extreme ability to organize a room, and make it look like the "before" and "after" pictures you see in all the magazines. To you, that may not be much.

To someone who can't walk through the front door of their house without stepping over piles of clothes, you are a superhero. Or how about the fact that you may have the ability to keep the peace in a room full of people who are insistent on being at each other's throat about something no one can even remember. You may have the gift of negotiation, where some people have no clue as to how to come to the table and reach a mutual agreement with another person, without arguing, fighting or name calling. Whatever your gift, know that it was designed with you in mind. Your gift doesn't have to be singing or acting or playing basketball or crunching seven-figure numbers. Your talent can be bringing calm to a chaotic situation. Your talent can be the ability to smile through adversity. Your gift may be sharing your story of heartache and triumph to a room full of women who have experienced your same pain, and have now lost hope. You may have the gift of leaving them happy, hopeful, and ready to face the world again. Never downplay your gift from God. Celebrate it for the unique hand-chosen, perfect gift that it is. God chose you to be the good steward of whatever gifts He gave you. As the rightful owner, it is a perfect opportunity for you to take the time to explore, understand, and operate in your gift(s). Learn to love and celebrate what God has gifted you.

# E

# You are ENOUGH

**Imperfectly Perfect.** You are strategically created, flaws included. Perfectly imperfect, that's what you are. Everything about you is exactly the way it needs to be. Even the things you see as flaws, make you even more unique and more beautiful. There is no such thing as a perfect person. There should be no beauty standard that dictates beauty for everyone. The enemy's

THE E.M.B.R.A.C.E. FORMULA

ploy is to get you to believe that if you don't look like the supermodel on TV (or the mother down the street who has 7 kids, but always seems to step out of her sports car picture-perfect, every hair in place, manicured nails, and the latest fashions... get my point?), then you don't measure up, and are somehow flawed beyond measure. Don't fall for the okie-doke. Remember, Satan is good at what he does and he won't quit until he has you believing that you are a mere nothing to not only the people around you, like your family and friends, but to God. In order to change your perception of how you see yourself, you have to get into the habit of celebrating everything about yourself, and that even means the "flaws" that Satan always reminds you of, every time he makes a suggestion in your ear. Don't only Celebrate your skin tone, celebrate your stretch marks. Don't just celebrate your hair when it's long, celebrate your beautiful bald head after a chemo treatment. Don't just celebrate losing 30 pounds and feeling slimmer and pretty, celebrate those extra pounds around your middle because beauty comes in ALL sizes. Celebrate your stutter, celebrate your crooked nose, celebrate your uneven toes. Celebrate all of you.

**#AllMistakesMatter** Your past qualifies you for your purpose. You are one of a kind, and so is your story. Your story is not only made up of the good, but the bad also. When you tell your story, it may be very tempting to leave out all of your mistakes, bad decisions, and the things you feel make you unworthy, unlovable and an awful person. But you must understand it is those things that you didn't get right the first time in life, that make you the beautiful person that you are now. If not for those tough times and mistakes, you would have never learned the lessons that you needed to learn. Your life lessons make for a powerful, and much needed testimony that so many others will benefit from. All of your stories matter... the good, the bad and the ugly. I believe that the more difficulties you face, the stronger you emerge from the rubble. Trials lead to tests, tests turn into triumphs, and triumphs turn into testimonies, which help bring about healing to others when shared. When things seem to be their worst in your life, that's when the enemy feels he has you right where he wants you...in a place of doom, gloom and defeat. It's a place where, more than likely, you will make lots of mistakes, feel insecure, and develop multi-levels of "stinkin-thinkin". The truth is the more mistakes you make, and the negative feelings you begin to feel about yourself don't have to last always. When you are in the "pit" of life, the lessons learned from that experience shape who you are, and help transform you into the "You", you are destined to be. And though it may not feel necessary at the time, your experiences, mistakes, and decisions, all work out in the end, for your good.

**Victor not Victim** - None of your tears or trials will go wasted. No one can tell your story like you can. No one. Not your mother, not your father, nor your spouse, has the ability to tell your story. It's as unique as you are, and it makes it's most impact when it's told by the one who starts out the VICTIM in the story, and later triumphs to become the VICTOR in the story. That person in you. You are the star of the story someone needs to hear. Their very life depends on it. Only when you tell your own story, can someone see the glory of God in your personal testimony. Everything that you have experienced, has brought you to such a time as this. When you lost your job, only to find and be hired for another job a year later, it prepared you to witness to the young woman who had just lost her job. When you were homeless with your child for over a year, and had no one to turn to, it prepared you to share your story and bless a woman who is living in a women's shelter and feeling alone and defeated. When you lost your child, and never thought you would smile again or get out of bed to face another day, it prepared you to turn to God, who soon blessed you with the opportunity to share your love with a child who had been abandoned by their family.

You are a child of God, so when times get hard, you have to remember that YOU WIN. You win because God never allows things to happen in our life "just because". Everything that happens, happens for a reason, and it is a strategic and intentional move on God's part. Never fear, God always has a plan, and it all will work out for your good.

**You are THE BOMB.COM**! You are beautifully and wonderfully made. (Psalm

139:14) You must believe how awesome you are. You are a beloved child of God. There will never ever be another like you. You are a one and only. Everything about you is totally unique. There has never been anyone like you, and there will never be. God literally broke the mold when he lovingly, and intentionally created you. God loves variety and diversity. The evidence of that can be seen just by watching the many people walk around in a crowded mall. You will see so many unique and beautifully made people. There are too many to count, and you will never, ever see any two alike. The Bible says in Psalm 139:13-14 NLT:

"You made all the delicate, inner parts of my body and knit me together in my mother's womb. Thank you for making me so wonderfully complex! Your workmanship is marvelous. How well I know it."

God doesn't make xerox copies. He's never had to reuse DNA, voice patterns, fingerprints, or footprints to create someone else. He has never run out ideas for a new human "model". You are one of a kind. You are special to Him, and you matter. He created you for a purpose, on purpose. You are not an accident. You aren't just a biological result of your mother and father getting together. God has a purposed plan for your life. God makes no mistakes. He created you for a specific reason. You aren't just a mere result of happenstance or random ideas. You were created intentionally, for a reason. Now, what that reason is, is for you to find out. The Bible is clear on one thing for sure: We were created to worship Him, and we can worship Him by giving thanks for who He is that created us.

# Conclusion

You did it! You made it to the end, and I want to congratulate you for making the decision to take your life, emotions, and thoughts back from the hands of your enemy. I challenge you to commit to applying to your life, everything you have learned from my story, and the chapters in this book. Please know that my prayer is that you have discovered that you can embrace your entire life and see its beauty through God's eyes. I pray you boldly face the enemy, look him square in the eye, and COMMAND him to get out of your thoughts, and never return.

Please enjoy my gift to you, a journal/workbook of the affirmations mentioned in this book.

bit.ly/Affirmations320

# ABOUT THE AUTHOR

I am Dorissa McCalister-Carnell, and I am known in these internet streets as "That Perception Chick".

I am an Inspirational Speaker, Amazon #1 International Best-Selling Author, singer, podcast host, and "Perception Coach".

I am the Founder and CEO of "God's Chosen Vessels", "God's Brats" and "Get WAISTed 4 Life".

I encourage women who are overwhelmed with life's surprises, traumas and disappointments, to see their life through God's eyes.

I have thrived in spite of molestation, homelessness, rape, bankruptcy, physical and mental abuse, the murder of my Daddy, my Momma living with Alzheimer's, a daughter born with mental and physical disorders, and divorce. I praise God for my testimony...To God Be The Glory!!

www.ingramcontent.com/pod-product-compliance
Lightning Source LLC
Chambersburg PA
CBHW072157090426
42740CB00012B/2296